C000041681

About this Learning Guide

Shmoop Will Make You a Better Lover*
*of Literature, History, Poetry, Life...

Our lively learning guides are written by experts and educators who want to show your brain a good time. Shmoop writers come primarily from Ph.D. programs at top universities, including Stanford, Harvard, and UC Berkeley.

Want more Shmoop? We cover literature, poetry, bestsellers, music, US history, civics, biographies (and the list keeps growing). Drop by our website to see the latest.

www.shmoop.com

Table of Contents

Introduction

In a Nutshell

In the 1960s, John F. Kennedy and Richard Nixon both won the presidency in part by positioning themselves as fierce anticommunist Cold Warriors. Once in office, however, both presidents found their ambitions of rolling back worldwide Communism thwarted by the threat of apocalyptic nuclear war. In the nuclear age, direct confrontation with the Soviet Empire simply became too dangerous to contemplate—a fact dramatized with terrifying clarity by the 1962 Cuban Missile Crisis. By the early 1970s, President Nixon—who had built his entire political career upon the principle of anticommunism—led a shift in American policy away from confrontation with the Soviet Union and toward détente, a policy of mutual acceptance and peaceful coexistence.

Why Should I Care?

Humankind has never come as close to apocalypse as it did in October 1962, when the United States and the Soviet Union found themselves locked in stalemate over nuclear missiles being installed in Cuba. For thirteen days, the world teetered on the brink. Finally, the Soviets relented and agreed to remove their missiles from the island. "We're eyeball to eyeball," said the American Secretary of State, "and I think the other fellow just blinked." Doomsday was averted, and Americans emerged from their backyard fallout shelters full of admiration for President John F. Kennedy, who had held his nerve with icy coolness to prevail in the standoff.

But everything Americans thought they understood about the Cuban Missile Crisis was wrong. Kennedy had not, in fact, prevailed through sheer resolve; he had defused the situation through negotiation and a secret compromise with the Soviet leadership. Kennedy's genius in the Missile Crisis was not truly his fearlessrefusal to bend to Soviet demands; to the contrary, it was his willingness to make a deal to avoid nuclear holocaust. But Kennedy's deal remained a secret, so most Americans learned exactly the wrong lesson from the crisis. Their determination to emulate Kennedy's supposed uncompromising resolve would not serve them well in Vietnam.

The true story is here. So is the story of how a ping-pong team changed the global geopolitical landscape.

What's not to like about that?

In Depth

Big Picture

From Confrontation to Détente

By the dawn of the 1960s, the Cold War was more than a decade old. Neither the containment doctrine of the Democratic Truman administration (1945-53) nor the "massive retaliation" policy of the Republican Eisenhower government (1953-61) had brought the United States close to victory over the Soviet Union. At the same time, neither had allowed Soviet Communists to conquer the globe, either. A tense stalemate was the order of the day.

In 1960, liberal Democratic Senator John F. Kennedy ran for president as a staunch Cold Warrior, promising to escalate America's global competition with the Soviets. Taking advantage of public fears that the US might be losing the Cold War, Kennedy positioned himself to the right of Republican World War II hero Dwight Eisenhower by building his campaign around a promise to close the "missile gap" that Eisenhower had supposedly allowed the Soviets to build up. (In fact, there was no "missile gap"; the US possessed always possessed several times as many nuclear missiles as their Soviet rivals. But the fake "missile gap" issue made for good politics, and Kennedy ran with it.) Kennedy's image as a tough but idealistic foe of Communism helped him to win the 1960 election by the narrowest of margins over Eisenhower's vice president, Richard Nixon.

In his inaugural address, Kennedy used soaring rhetoric to stake out a strong anticommunist position: "Let every nation know, whether it wishes us well or ill, that we shall pay any price, bear any burden, meet any hardship, support any friend, oppose any foe, in order to assure the survival and the success of liberty." Kennedy asked his countrymen to support his assertive but principled anticommunist vision, calling upon Americans to "ask not what your country can do for you; ask what you can do for your country."

Kennedy's muscular and idealistic anticommunist policy soon ran aground, however, in Cuba. A year before Kennedy took office, the Caribbean island—located just 90 miles off the coast of Florida—became the scene of a socialist revolution led by Fidel Castro. Castro, a charismatic young leftist, led a ragtag band of guerilla fighters to victory over the unloved Cuban dictator, Fulgencio Batista. While Castro antagonized and infuriated the traditional Cuban elite (many of whom soon fled to Florida), he won the affection and enthusiasm of a large majority of the impoverished Cuban people. The troubling popularity of the left-wing Castro regime presented a major problem to Kennedy's idealistic anticommunist vision; if the Cuban people supported Castro, could the United States then crush Castro's pro-Communist regime without betraying the principle of self-determination that Americans traditionally promised to defend?

Perhaps underestimating Castro's popularity in Cuba, Kennedy chose to seek his overthrow. Only a few months after becoming president, Kennedy authorized a CIA-organized force of anti-Castro Cuban exiles to invade Cuba. The ill-fated invaders landed at a place called the Bay of Pigs, where Castro's forces were waiting to crush them. The invasion failed to topple Castro's government and only strengthened his mystique among the Cuban people. The botched Bay of Pigs Invasion was a huge embarrassment to the United States; Kennedy took full responsibility for the debacle, but the defeat tarnished his reputation, making him appear both inept and unprincipled on the world stage.

A year later, events in Cuba again plunged the Kennedy administration—and this time the entire world—into crisis. When an American spy plane snapped pictures of Soviet troops installing nuclear missiles in Cuba, Kennedy publicly demanded their immediate removal and ordered a naval blockade of the island. Though his military advisers recommended on several occasions that Kennedy launch air strikes against the missile installations—air strikes which we now know would have almost certainly have led to nuclear war—Kennedy frantically pursued a strategy of negotiation with Soviet Premier Nikita Khrushchev. For thirteen long, tense days, the two great superpowers faced off in stalemate. Never before or since has the world teetered so close to nuclear apocalypse. The crisis finally ended when Kennedy and Khrushchev made a secret deal; in exchange for the Soviets backing down and withdrawing their missiles, the United States would remove its own nuclear missiles from Turkey and promise not to invade Cuba.

The near-death experience of the Cuban Missile Crisis spooked everyone, prompting a general shift in American policy away from directly challenging core Soviet interests. Soviet-American competition shifted to nonviolent venues (the space race and the Olympic games) or to peripheral areas of the world (Southeast Asia, the Middle East, southern Africa), where allies of the two superpowers fought each other in "proxy wars." These conflicts were certainly important (and tragically deadly), but they did not threaten the very existence of either the Soviet Union or the United States.

One of those proxy wars, in Vietnam, convulsed American society in the 1960s and destroyed the presidency of Kennedy's successor, Lyndon B. Johnson. Johnson's Vietnam-induced decision not to run for reelection in 1968 opened the door for the return of Kennedy's old foe from the 1960 election, Republican Richard Nixon. Nixon, like Kennedy, was a committed anticommunist. In fact, virtually his entire political had been built upon the reputation Nixon built as a crusading Communist-hunter during the Red Scare years of the late 1940s and early 1950s. As president, however, Nixon followed in Kennedy's post-Cuba footsteps by pursuing more moderate and nuanced policies towards the Soviet Union. Influenced by his powerful National Security Adviser, Henry Kissinger, Nixon came to see the Cold War as something more complex than a simple bipolar struggle between the US and USSR. Instead, Nixon embraced a multipolar world order in which Soviet and American interests would also be balanced by other nations. By cultivating relationships with other powerful nations—Communist China, Japan, France, Britain, Egypt—the United States could secure its global position.

The result was the Nixon/Kissinger policy of détente (a French word meaning "lessening of tension"), which by 1975 seemed to offer a future of mostly-peaceful coexistence between the superpowers. (In fact, the Cold War soon heated back up; by the 1980s détente was largely abandoned and confrontation once again became the order of the day.)

In retrospect, we can see the Kennedy-to-Nixon era as the "middle period" of the Cold War, falling after the uncertain early stages of the Truman/Eisenhower era but before the renewal of Soviet-American hostilities in the Carter/Reagan years. In this middle period, the clear historical trajectory (after the Cuban Missile Crisis) was away from confrontation and toward détente. In the Kennedy/Nixon era, American and Soviet leaders stared into the abyss of nuclear holocaust and chose to step back from the precipice.

Through the Lens of War

Is Arms Limitation MAD?

The arms race between the United States and the Soviet Union probably began as soon as the Soviets heard about the mushroom cloud over Hiroshima. In 1949, the Soviets—who had been working frantically to catch up with the Americans' nuclear technologies—detonated their first atomic bomb, and throughout the 1950s the two nations raced to build ever-growing stockpiles of nuclear weapons. By the 1960s, however, both sides began to question whether continuing to build their nuclear arsenals was really beneficial. Each country had enough weapons to destroy the other multiple times over—the US possessed around 30,000 nuclear warheads while the Soviets had about 5,000. Under President Dwight Eisenhower, Secretary of State John Foster Dulles had developed the policy of "massive retaliation," whereby nuclear weapons' real power was to deter attacks; Dulles reasoned that no nation would want to risk "massive retaliation" with nuclear weapons by attacking American interests abroad. President Lyndon Johnson's Secretary of State, Robert McNamara, built upon Dulles's ideas of deterrence to develop the policy of "Mutual Assured Destruction": if both Americans and Soviets adopted a policy of massive retaliation, and if both maintained a large enough nuclear arsenal to ensure each other's complete annihilation in the event of nuclear war, then the consequences of nuclear war would be so high that neither would ever launch a nuclear attack. Thus the Mutual Assured Destruction inherent in nuclear war would forever deter either side from ever starting one. Huge arsenals of nuclear weapons, paradoxically, were the only thing that could be depended upon to save the world from destruction by huge arsenals of nuclear weapons.

Many critics seized upon Mutual Assured Destruction's unfortunate acronym—MAD—to decry the policy a form of institutionalized madness, perpetuating a worldwide "balance of terror" that would forever threaten to end human civilization via nuclear holocaust. While the critics had a point—on several occasions since 1945 nuclear weapons have come terrifyingly close to being used, either by accident or miscalculation—anti-nuclear activists have never been able to develop a credible strategy for stuffing the nuclear genie back into the bottle. Mad as it may

have been, MAD did succeed in its most basic objective: the Soviet Union and United States never destroyed each other in nuclear war.

Surprisingly, perhaps, MAD led by the mid-1960s to the first successful nuclear arms control agreements. Once both sides possessed enough warheads to destroy each other completely, there was no need to continue racing to build ever-larger nuclear arsenals. After all, what was the point of being able to destroy the entire world many times over? After growing quickly throughout the 1950s and early 1960s, the American nuclear stockpile actually shrank slowly from a peak of 31,323 warheads in 1966 to 23,387 by 1980.

The Cuban Missile Crisis of 1962 demonstrated with horrifying clarity the dangers of nuclear proliferation (the spread of nuclear weapons to more and more countries). American President John F. Kennedy and Soviet Premier Nikita Khrushchev were able to stave off disaster through negotiation, but at the height of the crisis Cuban leader Fidel Castro actually pushed hard to launch a nuclear strike against the United States. If the weapons had been under Castro's operational control, rather than Khrushchev's, we might all be dead.

In 1963, in the immediate wake of the Missile Crisis, the leaders of the United States, Soviet Union, and Great Britain joined together to sign the Limited Test Ban Treaty, which they hoped would slow new development of nuclear weapons technology by banning test explosions in the atmosphere. More than 105 other nations signed on, though Cuba, China, and France all refused to join. While all three of those nations were allied with nuclear powers (the US in the case of France, the USSR in the case of Cuba and China), all three felt that only by controlling their own nuclear arsenals could they maintain their independence in world affairs.

France obtained the bomb in 1960, and China followed quickly after. While Chairman Mao had once dismissed the atom bomb as nothing more than a "paper tiger"—a weapon that looked fearsome but was worthless in battle—by the 1960s China desperately hoped to join the ranks of the nuclear powers. In 1964 Chinese scientists successfully detonated their first bomb.

The proliferation of nuclear technology to France and China only intensified American, British, and Soviet efforts to prevent even more countries from obtaining the bomb. In 1968, the United States, Great Britain, and the Soviet Union signed the Nuclear Non-Proliferation Treaty, agreeing not to distribute nuclear weapons to other nations and to limit the development of nuclear delivery systems. The treaty opened each country's nuclear facilities to inspections by the United Nations' International Atomic Energy Agency. The Nixon administration met with the Soviets in Helsinki, Finland, in 1969 to begin discussing further limits on nuclear weapons. These talks led to the 1972 Strategic Arms Limitation Treaty (SALT I), which froze the number of nuclear missiles (ICBMs) on both sides at current levels for five years. These agreements limiting nuclear weapons contributed greatly to détente (the relaxation of Cold War tensions) during this period. Nixon's successor as president, Gerald Ford, met with Khrushchev's successor, Leonid Brezhnev, in Siberia at Vladivostok to discuss more arms control. Ford laid the groundwork for SALT II, a second treaty which would be signed by Brezhnev and President

Jimmy Carterin Vienna a few years later.

Through the Lens of Diplomacy

Cuba: From Bay of Pigs to Missile Crisis

In 1959, the corrupt but pro-American dictatorship of Cuban President Fulgencio Batista collapsed, unable to survive the uprising of a ragtag army of guerillas led by a charismatic young leftist named Fidel Castro. Castro's overthrow of the unpopular Batista appalled some Cubans—especially members of the upper classes who had prospered under the Batista regime—but enthralled many more. Despite his many flaws, Castrobecame a beloved hero to a solid majority of the island nation's impoverished masses.

Castro's relationship with the United States was always going to be difficult. Though Castro's revolution was not sponsored by the Soviet Union and Castro himself was not even initially allied with the Cuban Communist Party, the young revolutionary's left-leaning Cuban nationalism caused alarm in Washington. American corporations had dominated the Cuban economy since the Spanish-American War at the turn of the twentieth century; Castro's insistence upon land reform—in 1960 he seized millions of acres owned by American companies and redistributed them to Cuban peasants—led to the United States imposing economic sanctions against Cuba. Castro, always eager to pick a fight with his neighbors to the north, retaliated by nationalizing Cuba's oil refineries and other American-owned businesses. The next round of tit-for-tat saw the Kennedy administration sever diplomatic relations with Cuba in 1961, an affront that led Castro to seek a formal alliance with America's archenemy, the Soviet Union.

Castro's alliance with Soviet Russia was simply unacceptable to American leaders. Previously, the Soviets had been able to expand the scope of their Communist sphere of influence in places in Eastern Europe and Asia, but never in "America's own backyard," the Western Hemisphere. Cuba lay just ninety miles off the coast of Florida. Castro's rise to power represented a major Cold War setback for the United States.

The Americans' solution was to attempt to overthrow the Castro regime. The CIA began training a band of anti-Castro Cuban exiles to lead an invasion against the island. The plan was for the exiles to land secretly at a place called the Bay of Pigs, then advance inland to rally a popular uprising to oust Castro's government. (The invasion's planners, Americans and Cuban exiles alike, wrongly assumed that the Cuban populace would back their efforts to depose Castro.) The Bay of Pigs invasion, launched in April 1961, proved to be a fiasco. The American-backed invaders, overpowered by Castro's army, never got off the beach. Their frantic pleas for support from the US Air Force were ignored, as President Kennedy refused to commit American forces to a direct attack against Cuba.

Kennedy, who had been in office for only three months, publicly accepted full responsibility for the Bay of Pigs debacle, which seemed to betray his idealistic principles even as it made him appear weak and impotent. The humiliation of the Bay of Pigs loomed large two months later, when the young president encountered Soviet Premier Nikita Khrushchev for the first time at the Vienna Summit. Khrushchev—an intimidating figure who once accentuated a speech at the United Nations by banging his shoe on a tabletop and on another occasion stunned Western diplomats by shouting,"We will bury you!"—took Kennedy for a lightweight and sought to bully him into acceding to Soviet demands. A startled Kennedy managed to stand firm on US policy at Vienna, but he was very unsettled by how weak the Bay of Pigs had made him look, and he became obsessed with plotting Castro's overthrow.

The CIA began scheming to assassinate the Cuban leader. (The most memorable of the CIA's many failed attempts to take Castro's life involved an exploding cigar.) More menacingly, the Pentagon conducted several military exercises in the Caribbean, practicing for the armed overthrow of a hypothetical foreign leader unsubtly named Ortsac. (Yes, that's Castro spelled backwards.) These maneuvers led Soviet Premier Nikita Khrushchev to begin covertly placing nuclear missiles on Cuba to defend the government of his new ally. As the Americans had recently deployed their own missiles in Turkey—which is as close to Russia as Cuba is to the United States—Khrushchev wrongly assumed that the Cuban missiles would not be seen as a threatening provocation in the United States. (The Soviets already possessed plenty of missiles that could hit the American mainland, so the placement of the weapons in Cuba didn't fundamentally alter the strategic balance.)

But President Kennedy didn't see things that way. On 14 October 1962, an American U2 spy plane snapped aerial reconnaissance photos that revealed Soviet workers building missile bases on Cuba. In Washington, the top echelon of the American government went into crisis mode. President Kennedy canceled all scheduled public appearances, falsely claiming to have caught a bad cold. In fact he had convened a special committee of top advisers, called the ExComm, whose members spent long hours in tense debate over how the US should respond. Military leaders urged Kennedy to launch air strikes immediately to destroy the missile installations before they became operational, or to order a fell-fledged American invasion of Cuba to get rid of Castro once and for all. But Kennedy feared that such an escalation would lead to full-blown nuclear war. (And subsequent revelations from post-Cold War Soviet archives reveal that Kennedy was almost certainly correct.) Instead of attacking Cuba, Kennedy determined to negotiate with the Soviets to ensure the missiles' removal. But he intended to negotiate from a position of strength, and to do that he needed to raise the stakes.

In a dramatic and somber televised address on 22 October, Kennedy informed the American people for the first time of the presence of Soviet missiles in Cuba and demanded their immediate removal. He also announced the imposition of a "quarantine" around Cuba to block further shipments of nuclear-related cargoes to the island. (The "quarantine" was actually a total American naval blockade, but since a blockade is officially an act of war under international law, Kennedy chose to call it a "quarantine" instead.) Kennedy also declared that any launch of

missiles from Cubawould be seen as a direct attack on the United States by the Soviet Union, and that he would respond by nuking Russia. The threat of full-fledged nuclear war had never been more imminent.

Two days later, Soviet ships carrying more missiles to add to those already installed in Cuba continued to steam toward the island. They approached the blockade line, showing no signs they planned to stop. The US Navy discovered they were accompanied by armed submarine escort. Would the Soviets attempt to breach the blockade line? Would the Americans use force to stop them? Would the confrontation end in nuclear war?

As the crew of the USS *Essex* began preparing to intercept the Soviet freighters, the missile-bearing ships suddenly came to a halt, then slowly turned around and began sailing away. "We're eyeball to eyeball," said American Secretary of State Dean Rusk, "and I think the other fellow just blinked."

While the Soviets may have blinked, the Cuban Missile Crisis wasn't over. The blockade may have prevented more missiles from reaching Cuba, but Kennedy still insisted that the missiles already emplaced on the island had to go. Khrushchev could not simply capitulate without undermining his own reputation and the prestige of the Soviet Union. Leaders in Washington and Moscow engaged in frantic, confused negotiations to try to resolve the standoff. The tension began to take a toll; on 26 October, Khrushchev sent an incoherent, rambling message to Kennedy, at one point writing, "Mr. President, Mr. Kennedy, you and I are like two men pulling on a rope with a knot in the middle, the harder we pull, the tighter the knot until it will have to be cut with a sword. Now why we don't both let up the pressure and maybe we can untie the knot?" Khrushchev offered to withdraw his missiles if the Kennedy would vow publicly not to invade Cuba. While the Kennedy administration was contemplating this offer, a new message arrived from Moscow proposing an entirely different deal: the Soviet Union would remove their missiles from Cuba only if the US removed its own Jupiter missiles from Turkey. The unexplained, contradictory offers spooked the ExComm, making Kennedy's advisers wonder whether Khrushchev was even still in charge in Moscow.

Meanwhile the crisis escalated once again as a Cuban surface-to-air missile shot down an American U2 spy plane that was continuing reconnaissance over the island. Ameican policy in the case of a downed U2 called for immediate destruction of the anti-aircraft site, but Kennedy pushed his generals to accept restraint. Castro, fearing imminent American attack, urged Khrushchev to strike against the US. Khrushchev too held back, waiting for Kennedy's response.

Kennedy's team was befuddled by the two different offers from Khrushchev and was uncertain how to respond. Robert F. Kennedy—the president's brother and Attorney General—suggested that the Americans write back, accepting the terms of Khrushchev's first offer while simply not mentioning the second letter. Meanwhile, the Robert Kennedy met secretly with Soviet Ambassador Anatoly Dobrynin, promising that the US would remove its Jupiter missiles from

Turkey if the Soviets took their missiles out of Cuba, but only on the condition that the Soviets never made the *quid pro quo* public. Kennedy did not want to appear to have given in to Soviet pressure or to have sold out his European allies. After thirteen long days of almost unbearable tension, the secret Kennedy/Dobrynin agreement brought the Cuban Missile Crisis to a peaceful conclusion.

The secrecy that surrounded the negotiations that ended the crisis allowed Kennedy to convey to the public the impression that he had prevailed through steely resolve in the face of Soviet pressure. Most Americans viewed the outcome of the Cuban Missile Crisis as an unalloyed triumph for John F. Kennedy, adding to the president's substantial mystique. The fact that disaster had actually been averted through negotiation and compromise would not become clear until much later. In the meantime, many Americans took their misconceptions of what had happened in the Missile Crisis as proof that they could prevail in Cold War confrontations by refusing to give an inch to their Communist foes. It was a dubious lesson that would not serve them well in Vietnam.

The mutual terror caused by the Cuban Missile Crisis convinced Kennedy and Khrushchev that they needed to improve communication between the two nations to ensure that such a dangerous misunderstanding never happened again. They set up the famous hotline between their offices to allow for direct contact in times of crisis, and they signed the Limited Test Ban Treaty to slow the arms race. Kennedy became convinced of the need to pursue a more nuanced policy towards the Soviet Union and to accept a certain level of Soviet domination of Eastern European affairs. However, Khrushchev suffered politically at home and among his allies for the humiliation of his apparent capitulation in Cuba. Other Soviet leaders and Soviet allies were embarrassed by the turn of events, and in 1964 Khrushchev was forced into retirement, replaced as Soviet leader by hardliner Leonid Brezhnev.

Prague Spring... and Fall

By the late 1960s, cracks began to appear in the Soviet Union's Iron Curtain. Eastern European Communists, who had been forced into the Soviet orbit following World War II, sought to bring greater freedoms to their Communist societies. In 1968, the new leader of Czechoslovakia's Communist Party, Alexander Dubcek, sought to enact a series of reforms to transform Czech Communism into "socialism with a human face," with greater freedom of expression than Soviet-dominated Czech regimes had previously allowed. Crowds of Czechs gathered in Prague to discuss the crimes of the past regimes and to learn about the new reforms. Two other relatively liberal and independent Communist leaders, Josip Tito of Yugoslavia and Nicolae Ceausescu of Romania, visited Dubcek to show their support. Students in Poland and Yugoslavia demonstrated in sympathy with the reformers' cause. The flowering of support for new freedom and openness in Czech society came to be known as the "Prague Spring." The Czech people soon began to push for even greater reforms than Dubcek had proposed, and the nation became divided as Dubcek urged caution and moderation while other leaders pushed for even more drastic change.

In Moscow, Soviet leaders began to worry that the spirit of reform in Czechoslovakia would spiral out of control, possibly carrying the country out of the Soviet orbit entirely. They feared that the mass enthusiasm for freedom unleashed by the Prague Spring might spread throughout Eastern Europe, threatening the Soviet stranglehold on that region. In the end, Soviet Premier Leonid Brezhnev sent in the Red Army to crush the Czechs' growing spirit of independence . Soviet tanks rolled through the streets of Prague. Czech leaders were flown to Moscow and forced to renounce their own reforms. Censorship returned to Czechoslovakia.

The Prague Spring of 1968 represented a brief moment of hope for Czechoslovakia and for the subjects of other Communist regimes behind the Iron Curtain. But that hope died with the Soviet invasion.

The American public was stunned by the invasion, which provided shocking images for display on the front pages of their newspapers and on their television screens. Nightly news broadcasts sympathized with the Czech reformers and vividly portrayed the brutality of the Soviet response with film smuggled out of Czechoslovakia. American scholars compared the Soviets' behavior to that of Adolf Hitler.

Balancing Power in Asia

Even as the Soviets sought to reimpose their control over Eastern Europe with an iron fist, they encountered new problems in Asia, where longtime ally Mao Zedong sought to make China, not Russia, the world's foremost Communist power.

By 1972, President Richard Nixon and his National Security Adviser Henry Kissinger saw an opportunity to divide China from Russia, allowing them to pursue a new, multipolar Cold War strategy. Communist China was eager to take its rightful place in world affairs, and Chairman Mao was irked by what he perceived as the Soviets' attitude of condescension toward his country. Mao had predicted the "East Wind rising over West Wind"—China (the East Wind) would surpass the Soviet Union (the West Wind) as the world's leading Communist nation. Meanwhile, the United States—reeling from defeat in Vietnam—sought to appear strong in foreign policy, giving the impression that the Vietnamese debacle did not mean a broader disaster for the US in the Cold War. If all went well, Nixon and Kissinger could exploit the Sino-Soviet split by playing China off the Soviet Union.

Nixon's approach to China marked a dramatic reversal of American policy toward the world's most populous nation. Since 1949, the official American position regarding Red China had been that it did not exist. (In 1949, the Chinese Civil War ended with Mao's Communists taking control of the entire mainland, while Chiang Kai-Shek's Nationalists fled to the island province of Taiwan. Thereafter both the Communists in Beijing and the Nationalists in Taipei claimed to be the legitimate government of all of China—both mainland and Taiwan. The United States continued to recognize Chiang's Taiwan as the legitimate government of all of China, allowing the Nationalists to hold China's powerful permanent seat on the United Nations Security Council until 1972.)

In a strange twist, China opened up the possibility of rapprochement by inviting the American ping-pong team—then playing in Japan—to visit the country in the spring of 1971. The team's nine players, along with some of their spouses and a few officials and journalists, were the first Americans given official sanction to enter China since the Communists gained control of the mainland more than twenty years before. Tim Boggan, one of the American officials for the ping-pong team, later recalled the odd juxtaposition of being greeted with smiles from the Chinese team and diplomats while seeing Chinese propaganda posters that portrayed caricatures of a pygmy Nixon alongside slogans such as "Down with the US imperialists and all their running dogs!"[1] The Americans may have lost their exhibition matches against China's talented table tennis players, but they won much goodwill in China by meeting with students and workers and touring the Great Wall. Back in the United States, Americans were enthralled by newspaper and television reports on the team's "ping-pong diplomacy." *Time* magazine called it "the ping heard round the world."[2] Chinese Premier Zhou Enlai said to the US team, "You have opened a new chapter in the relations of the American and Chinese people. I am confident that this beginning again of our friendship will certainly meet with majority support of our two peoples."[3] Surely ping-pong has never before or since served such a vital diplomatic function.

The United States responded to "ping-pong diplomacy" by sending Henry Kissinger to China in July 1971 to lay the groundwork for Nixon to travel there later. Kissinger kept his own mission a secret so that Nixon could surprise the world by announcing the first-ever presidential visit to Communist China. Nixon's journey in February 1972 drew attention away from the war in Vietnam and towards a positive relationship with China. The United States recognized Communist China's existence and reversed its longstanding resistance to admitting the country to the United Nations, and after Mao's death in 1976, his successor Deng Xiaoping finalized a formal agreement to restore diplomatic relations between the two nations. China took over Taiwan's seat on the Security Council .

While any other American leader would have been sharply criticized for considering diplomacy with China, Nixon's lifelong reputation as a ferocious Cold Warrior was so strong that people found it difficult to charge him with going "soft on Communism." Having built his political career on targeting suspected communists in the government, Nixon's anticommunist credentials were unassailable and certainly beyond those of any preceding president. It's ironic, then, that the most hardline American president of the Cold War era was the only one who could open the United States to friendship with Communist China. "Only Nixon could go to China" has since become almost an American political cliché.

Through the Lens of Economy

Cuba

The United States had maintained a strong presence in Cuba ever since it helped Cuba gain its independence in the Spanish-American War of 1898. American businesses began to invest heavily in Cuba and expected a government friendly to their interests. During the 1930s, however, the Cuban government took a more nationalistic turn and promoted greater Cuban control of the economy. In response to this threat against American interests, officials in Washington helped to establish the dictatorship of Fulgencio Batista, who took a permissive attitude toward continued American dominance of the Cuban economy—from natural resources to nightlife. With Batista in power, wealthy Americans and even American mobsters came to see Cuba as their personal playground. But even as Batista's regime won support from Americans, his harsh policies and uncompromising dictatorship turned many of the Cuban people against him.

Guerrillas, first in the mountains and then in the towns, began attacking government buildings and the army as early as 1953. Led by the charismatic young Fidel Castro, these guerrillas eventually succeeded in leading a revolution that toppled Batista's government in 1959. Castro became, for most Cubans, a national hero, cementing his role as the new leader of Cuba. Castro began to institute land reform, nationalizing millions of acres owned by American companies and seizing control of the country's businesses and natural resources from foreign investors. In response, the United States severed diplomatic relations with Cuba in 1961, leading Cuba to ally itself with the Soviet Union.

Castro was both a leftist and an ardent Cuban nationalist, and it would have been very difficult for the United States to maintain good relations with his regime under any circumstances. That said, it is important to note that Castro did not seize power in Cuba in the name of the Communist Party; he did not fully embrace Communism until he had been ruling Cuba for more than two years, and even then his alliance with the Soviet Empire came about only in the wake of American sanctions against his regime. Did those sanctions, imposed largely to protect the interests of large American corporations whose interests were threatened by Castro's nationalistic economic policies, push Castro into the Soviet orbit? Critics of American foreign policy have long asserted that the US government's unbending support for American corporations' narrow interests in Cuba amounted to a kind of economic imperialism that practically drove Castro into alliance with the Soviets, thus undermining broader American Cold War strategic interests.

Oil in the Middle East

While Cuba was economically important to a handful of powerful American companies, the Middle East provided a vital resource—oil—that was critical to the entire American economy. US policy in the Middle East had the difficult task of balancing America's interest in that oil with

America's traditional support for Israel, which usually had hostile relations with the neighboring nations that controlled the oil. In 1960, a number of those Middle Eastern nations joined together to form the Organization of Petroleum Exporting Countries (OPEC). The Middle Eastern states of Iraq, Iran, Kuwait, and Saudi Arabia, plus the South American nation of Venezuela, sought to use the organization to coordinate petroleum production and pricing.

These nations watched closely during the Six Day War of 1967 and the Yom Kippur War of 1973, both of which pitted Israel (backed by the United States) against Egypt and Syria (backed by the Soviet Union). In the 1967 conflict, Israel launched a preemptive strike against its Arab neighbors, storming to victory and seizing expansive new territories in the West Bank, Golan Heights, and Sinai Peninsula. Six years later, Egypt and Syria struck back with a surprise attack launched on the Jewish holiday of Yom Kippur. Arab armies pushed into Israel, recapturing much of the ground lost in 1967. The Americans, assuming incorrectly that the Soviets were behind the Arab attack, responded to Israel's pleas for aid with a massive airlift of supplies that helped to turn the tide of the war.

OPEC responded to America's intervention on Israel's behalf by placing an embargo on oil sales to the United States and raising oil prices around the world. The embargo would continue through 1974, quadrupling the price of oil in the United States. For the first time since World War II, Americans endured gasoline rationing. In some areas, people whose cars carried license plates ending in odd numbers purchased gas on odd days of the month, while those with license plates ending in even numbers purchased gas on even days of the month. (To keep it fair, everyone could purchase gas on the 31st.)

The Oil Crisis made clear to American policymakers the costs of supporting Israel in a hostile Middle East. It also brought the attention of the American public away from the Nixon administration's successes with the Soviet Union and China to the problems of policy in the Third World. The thorny interrelationship of America's strategic and economic interests in the Middle East would continue to bedevil American policymakers into the twenty-first century.

Through the Lens of Science & Technology

The Missile Gap

John F. Kennedy campaigned for president in 1960 by claiming that the Eisenhower administration had allowed the Soviet Union to open up a "missile gap" on the United States. At a 1960 speech in Florida, Kennedy stoked fears of Cold War inferiority. "We are moving into a period," he said, "when the Soviet Union will be outproducing us two or three to one in the field of missiles—a period relatively vulnerable and when our retaliatory force will be in danger of destruction through a Soviet surprise attack—the period of the missile gap."Kennedy used the "missile gap" issue to position himself as a candidate even more hawkish than his opponent,

Vice President Richard Nixon (who was himself a staunch Cold Warrior).

Kennedy's charges seemed credible. The Soviet Union had succeeded in developing the world's first intercontinental ballistic missile (ICBM) in 1957. The ICBM could travel farther than any other previous technology—the test missile soared 4,000 miles across the Pacific—thus making it possible to hit targets from much farther away. The Soviets used one of those missiles to launch Sputnik, the first satellite to orbit the earth.

Americans panicked, fearing that the Soviets' new long-range missiles could hit the US mainland if launched from the Russian coast. The American government raced to develop its own ICBM, the Atlas, and finally succeeded in 1959. American analysts assumed that the Soviets had used their two-year head start to build up a huge stockpile of ICBMs. The American media reported estimates that within a few years the Soviet Union would possess 1,000 ICBMs and the United States only 70.[5] In fact, the Soviets had only built a handful of missiles. By the time Kennedy took office in 1961, CIA surveillance revealed that there was indeed a missile gap—but it favored the United States. The Soviets had only 10 intercontinental ballistic missiles to the Americans' 57.

Timeline

January 2, 1959

Castro in Cuba
In Cuba, a charismatic young leftist named Fidel Castro leads his guerilla forces triumphantly into Havana, toppling the government of Fulgencio Batista. While most Cubans initially celebrate Castro's victory over the unpopular, corrupt Batista, Americans fear that Castro will establish a Soviet-friendly regime just 90 miles off the Florida coast.

April 1959

Castro Tours US
New Cuban leader Fidel Castro tours the United States, hiring a prominent American PR firm to coordinate a charm offensive in hopes of reassuring Americans that the new revolutionary government in Cuba poses no threat to the United States. While Castro receives some positive coverage in the American press, President Dwight Eisenhower refuses to meet with him.

February 1960

Cuba and US Sever Ties

Fidel Castro negotiates a trade agreement with the Soviet Union, allowing Cuba to import Soviet oil. Cuba's refineries—all owned by American corporations—refuse to process the Soviet crude, and Castro retaliates by nationalizing the refineries. Castro's seizure of this American property leads to the severing of diplomatic relations between the United States and Cuba.

June 1960

Cuban Sugar Quota Cut

The Eisenhower administration cuts Cuba's sugar quota, depriving Cuba of the opportunity to sell 7 million tons of sugar (one of Cuba's most important exports) in the American market. Castro threatens to nationalize all American-owned property in Cuba in retaliation.

September 14, 1960

OPEC Founded

OPEC (the Organization of Petroleum Exporting Countries) is founded by Iraq, Iran, Kuwait, Saudi Arabia, and Venezuela to coordinate petroleum production and pricing.

August 7, 1960

Cuba Nationalizes American Property

Fidel Castro follows through on his threat to nationalize all American-owned property in Cuba. Lands and businesses worth more than $850 million become the property of the Cuban government.

October 18, 1960

The Missile Gap

Presidential candidate John F. Kennedy, Democratic Senator from Massachusetts, argues that the Eisenhower administration has allowed a "missile gap" to develop between the United States and the Soviet Union. He claims that the Soviets are outpacing the United States in missile production, and that he will reverse this gap if elected. (In fact, there is no missile gap;

the United States possesses several times as many missiles as the Soviets.)

November 8, 1960

Kennedy Elected
Democratic Senator John F. Kennedy of Massachusetts is elected president, narrowly defeating Republican Vice President Richard Nixon in the 1960 elections.

January 20, 1961

Kennedy Inaugurated
President John F. Kennedy's inaugural address showcases the young president's idealism. Even while demonstrating his commitment to the Cold War by promising that he will not shrink from defending freedom, he also promises to be open to cooperation with the Soviet Union in the interest of peace and arms control: "Let us never negotiate out of fear," he says. "But let us never fear to negotiate. Let both sides explore what problems unite us instead of belaboring those problems which divide us."

March 13, 1961

Alliance for Progress
President John F. Kennedy launches the Alliance for Progress, a massive program of economic aid for the Western Hemisphere akin to the earlier Marshall Plan for Western Europe. Kennedy hopes the Alliance will generate economic growth and social progress in the developing nations of Latin America, inspiring allegiance to the United States while making Communism a less attractive alternative.

March 1, 1961

Peace Corps
President John F. Kennedy establishes the Peace Corps to send idealistic young Americans to aid developing countries around the world. Kennedy hopes the organization will create positive feelings towards the United States in Africa and Asia while undermining the appeal of anti-American revolutionary movements.

July 9, 1961

No Cities/Counterforce
Hoping to make the use of nuclear weapons more feasible, Defense Secretary Robert
McNamara proposes the strategy of "no cities/counterforce," which would target Soviet military
bases instead of cities in order to lower the number of potential casualties.

April 12, 1961

Soviet Becomes First Man in Space
The USSR's Yuri Gagarin becomes the first man in space, successfully completing one orbit
around earth in his Vostok 1 spacecraft.

April 17, 1961

Bay of Pigs
A CIA-organized force of anti-Castro Cuban exiles attempts to invade Cuba, landing at a place
called the Bay of Pigs. Rather than toppling Castro's government, the invasion is quickly
crushed by Cuba's armed forces. President Kennedy takes full responsibility for the debacle.

June 4, 1961
Vienna SummitPresident John F. Kennedy meets with Soviet Premier Nikita Khrushchev at the
Vienna Summit. Khrushchev attempts to intimidate the inexperienced Kennedy, using the
president's humiliation in the Bay of Pigs fiasco to bully him into accepting East German
demands that would cut off Western access to Berlin. But Kennedy stands firm on defending
West Berlin, and his closing words to Khrushchev promise "a cold winter."

August 12, 1961

East Germans Isolated
East Germany closes the border between East and West Berlin in an attempt to cut off East
Germans' flight to the more prosperous West.

August 15, 1961

Berlin Wall

East Germany builds the Berlin wall, dividing East and West Berlin. The wall separates families, cuts off workers from jobs, and devastates Berliners on both sides, becoming the most powerful symbol of the oppression of Eastern Europe under Soviet domination.

October 27, 1961

Checkpoint Charlie

American and Soviet tanks face off for two days at Checkpoint Charlie, one of the few border crossings remaining between East and West Berlin following East Germany's closure of the border. After East German police violate an agreement allowing free transport of diplomats across Berlin's sectors, American general Lucius Clay sends in diplomats to test the East German response. After one of these tests, Soviet tanks menacingly approach the border; Clay calls out his tanks to meet them. The confrontation is only resolved when Soviet Premier Nikita Khrushchev and President John F. Kennedy negotiate a deal: the Soviet tanks will back down if Kennedy will not protest the construction of the Berlin Wall.

October 30, 1961

Tsar Bomb

A Russian bomber drops the Tsar bomb, the largest nuclear weapon ever detonated, in a test over the Arctic Ocean. The 57-megaton Tsar bomb is thousands of times more powerful than the atomic bomb dropped on Hiroshima in 1945.

November 30, 1961

Operation Mongoose

President John F. Kennedy initiates the CIA's Operation Mongoose, authorizing covert attempts to overthrow Fidel Castro's communist regime in Cuba. Operation Mongoose is a failure and pushes Castro closer to the Soviet Union.

October 14, 1962

Cuban Missile Crisis

The Cuban Missile Crisis begins after American U2 surveillance flights confirm that the Soviets have placed nuclear missiles on Cuba. President John F. Kennedy rejects advice from military advisors to launch an immediate attack on Cuba.

October 22, 1962

Cuba Quarantine

President John F. Kennedy goes on national television to announce the presence of Soviet missiles on Cuba and the imposition of an American "quarantine" or naval blockade around Cuba. Kennedy begins negotiations with Soviet Premier Nikita Khrushchev, largely leaving Cuban leader Fidel Castro out of the loop.

October 28, 1962

Cuban Missile Crisis Resolved

The Cuban Missile Crisis ends after President Kennedy and Premier Khrushchev reach a secret agreement: the Soviet Union agrees to remove its missiles from Cuba if the Americans will remove its own Jupiter missiles from Turkey (which is about as far from the USSR as Cuba is from the US). The deal is kept secret from the public, which believes that Kennedy has won his victory through pure resolve rather than through negotiation.

August 5, 1963

Limited Test Ban Treaty

The United States, Soviet Union, and Great Britain sign the Limited Test Ban Treaty, which bans atmospheric nuclear tests in hopes of slowing the arms race and protecting against nuclear fallout.

November 22, 1963

Johnson Presidency

Lyndon Baines Johnson assumes the presidency after the assassination of President John F. Kennedy. "I will do my best," Johnson says, in his first public statement as president. "That is all I can do. I ask for your help, and God's."

June 16, 1963

First Woman in Space
Soviet cosmonaut Valentina Vladimirovna Tereshkova makes the first flight by a woman in space.

June 20, 1963

Hotline Established
The American and Soviet governments set up a telephone hotline to ensure that the two country's leaders will always be able to establish direct communications during future Cold War crises.

November 1, 1963

Vietnam Coup
South Vietnamese leader Ngo Dinh Diem, a corrupt and unpopular ruler, is killed in a military coup carried out with US approval. Rather than improving the situation, Diem's murder plunges South Vietnam even deeper into crisis.

1964

Mutually Assured Destruction
Defense Secretary Robert McNamara develops the idea of Mutual Assured Destruction, which holds that in a world in which both the US and USSR possess enough nuclear weapons to wipe each other off the map, both sides' fears of nuclear retaliation will prevent either from ever using the weapons for aggressive purposes. Thus nuclear weapons are the best deterrent against nuclear war. Although critics decry McNamara's nuclear "balance of terror" policy as mad (MAD, conveniently, is the acronym for Mutual Assured Destruction), McNamara believes his policy will help maintain a stable nuclear world.

August 2, 1964

Gulf of Tonkin Incident

In the Tonkin Gulf, off the coast of Vietnam, the Communist North Vietnamese allegedly attack American ships that have strayed near Vietnamese waters. The "Gulf of Tonkin Incident" gives the Johnson administration a pretext to justify sending American troops to intervene in Vietnam.

August 7, 1964

Gulf of Tonkin Resolution

Congress passes the Gulf of Tonkin Resolution by a unanimous vote in the House and a nearly unanimous vote of 88-2 in the Senate, giving President Lyndon Johnson the authority to send American troops to Vietnam and to use "all necessary measures to repel armed attack."

October 16, 1964

Chinese Atomic Bomb

Communist China detonates its first successful atomic bomb.

October 14, 1964

Leonid Brezhnev Rules

Leonid Brezhnev replaces Nikita Khrushchev as First Secretary of the Communist Party. Brezhnev will rule the Soviet Union until 1982.

November 3, 1964

Johnson Landslide

In the 1964 presidential election, Democrat Lyndon B. Johnson crushes Republican Barry Goldwater to win a second term as president.

May 16, 1966

Cultural Revolution

Chinese leader Mao Zedong initiates the Cultural Revolution, which aims to renew support for revolutionary Communism and rid Chinese society of bourgeois elements. In support, some Chinese students launch the Red Guards, an anarchic and sometimes violent student movement against party leaders and intellectuals who do not fully support Mao and his policies. China comes close to civil war with massive purges of intellectuals and political opponents. Estimates of the number of people killed in the Cultural Revolution range from 500,000 to 3 million. The Cultural Revolution lasts a decade and brings higher education in China to a halt.

June 5, 1967

Six Day War
Israel battles Egypt in the Six Day War. After the Israelis launch a pre-emptive strike upon learning that Egypt is contemplating war, triumphant Israeli forces seize Sinai and the Gaza Strip from Egypt, the West Bank and East Jerursalem from Jordan, and the Golan Heights from Syria. The fighting surprises the US government.

July 1, 1968

Nuclear Non-Proliferation Treaty
The United States, Soviet Union, and Great Britain (among other nations) sign the Nuclear Non-Proliferation Treaty, agreeing not to spread nuclear weapons to other countries and to limit nuclear delivery systems. The treaty gives the United Nations' International Atomic Energy Agency the job of inspecting nuclear facilities.

July 25, 1969

Nixon Doctrine
The Nixon Doctrine of President Richard Nixon states that the United States will continue to lend support to its allies with money and weaponry, but will largely leave them responsible for manning their own defenses.

January 5, 1968

Prague Spring
The Prague Spring begins when Alexander Dubcek replaces Antonin Novotny as general

secretary of the Communist Party of Czechoslovakia. Dubcek presses for reform, seeking to create a more open Communist society that he calls "socialism with a human face." Josip Tito of Yugoslavia and Nicolae Ceausescu of Romania visit Dubcek to show their support, and students in Poland and Yugoslavia protest in sympathy with Czechoslovakia. The Czech people soon demand even greater reforms, beyond those proposed by Dubcek's government. Dubcek, who counsels moderation, finds himself divided from other influential leaders.

August 21, 1968

Czechoslovakia Falls
Soviet forces invade Czechoslovakia, crushing the Prague Spring. Czech leaders are flown to Moscow, where they are forced to renounce their earlier reforms, leading to the reintroduction of censorship.

November 13, 1968

Brezhnev Doctrine
The Brezhnev Doctrine of Soviet Premier Leonid Brezhnev justifies repressing the Prague Spring reformers in Czechoslovakia by stating that no socialist state can adopt policies endangering the interests of international socialism, and that the Soviet Union can intervene in any Soviet-bloc nation if communist rule there is threatened.

November 5, 1968

Nixon Elected
Republican Richard Nixon defeats Democrat Hubert Humphrey and segregationist American Independent Party candidate George Wallace in the 1968 presidential election.

October 21, 1969

Chacellor Willy Brandt and Ostpolitik
Willy Brandt, the first West German Chancellor from the Social Democratic Party, becomes the first chancellor to visit East Germany and also begins *Ostpolitik*—recognizing East Germany as a state in order to improve relations within Germany.

November 17, 1969

SALT

A meeting in Helsinki, Finland, between the United States and Soviet Union initiates the first phase of a Strategic Arms Limitation Treaty (SALT), freezing both sides' number of ballistic missile launchers at current levels.

April 12, 1971

Ping Pong Diplomacy

The United States and China engage in "Ping Pong Diplomacy" as the US Table Tennis Team becomes the first officially-sanctioned group of Americans to set foot in Beijing since the Communist takeover in 1949.

September 4, 1970

Salvador Allende Becomes President of Chile

In Chile, leftist Salvador Allende heads a political coalition supported by both the ChileanSocialist and Communist parties. Despite CIA attempts to weaken his support, Allende is freely elected president, putting Marxists in power by democratic means. Allende nationalizes the country's vital copper industry, gives free milk to schoolchildren, and begins to put the economy under state control.

August 26, 1970

Cienfuegos Crisis

The Cienfuegos Crisis begins when an American U2 spy plane spots a submarine base in Cuba. The US wants the removal of Soviet missile submarines from Cuba, but fears that any public confrontation will escalate into a repeat of the Cuban Missile Crisis. Secretary of State Henry Kissinger thus chooses to handle the issue with quiet diplomacy.

February 1, 1970

Soviet-German Pipeline Agreed

The Soviet Union and West Germany make a deal, agreeing to build an oil pipeline between the two nations. These negotiations demonstrate West German leader Willy Brandt's strategy of showing his openness to working with the Soviets in order to build better relations with Soviet-controlled East Germany.

August 12, 1970

Moscow Treaty
In the Moscow Treaty, the USSR and West Germany agree to existing borders and to normalize relations between the two nations.

December 20, 1970

Polish Strikes
The Polish army violently puts down strikes of protesting workers in Gdansk, Poland. Communist Party leader Wladyslaw Gomulka resigns and is replaced by Edward Gierek.

May 26, 1972

Antiballistic Missile Treaty
The US and USSR sign the Antiballistic Missile Treaty to limit anti-ballistic missile systems, which could potentially defend against missiles carrying nuclear weapons. This treaty formalizes Mutual Assured Destruction.

May 3, 1971

East Open to Détente
East German leader Walter Ulbricht is forced out of power and is replaced by Erich Honecker, who is more open to détente with the West.

July 1971

Kissinger Tours Asia

Secretary of State Henry Kissinger tours Asia, secretly visiting Beijing to open up diplomatic relations with Communist China.

September 3, 1971

Four Powers Agreement Reached

The Four Power Agreement on Berlin between the four World War II allies—Britain, France, the United States, and Soviet Union—finally resolves critical issues created during the occupation of Germany in 1945. The Western powers agree to recognize East Berlin as the capital of East Germany and the Soviets agree to improve access between East and West Berlin.

February 21, 1972

Nixons Opens China

President Richard Nixon travels to China and meets Chinese leader Mao Zedong. This visit opens the door to rapprochement with China.

December 21, 1972

Basic Treaty Signed

West and East Germany sign the Treaty for the Basis of Relations (also known as the Basic Treaty), which gives East Germany *de facto* recognition of its statehood and borders though not *de jure* recognition. This means that while West German leader Willy Brandt is willing to recognize that East Germany operates as a sovereign state in practice, he is not willing to legally define East Germany as a separate from the German nation. Brandt adopts this stance because he hopes for the eventual reunification of Germany. This distinction between *de facto* and *de jure* recognition plays out in East and West Germany's exchange of permanent representatives rather than ambassadors.

May 22, 1972

Détente

President Richard Nixon travels to the USSR for a summit with Soviet Premier Leonid Brezhnev in the Kremlin. They agree to seek a policy of détente, neither seeking an advantage at the expense of the other.

May 29, 1972

SALT I Signed

The signing of the first Strategic Arms Limitation Treaty (SALT I) by the United States and USSR in Moscow heralds the beginning of détente. The treaty freezes the number of intercontinental ballistic missiles (ICBMs) held by each country for five years. The treaty also shows an acceptance of equal strategic arsenals—both the US and USSR realize that they each will continue to have a large number of weapons no matter how vigorously they compete in an arms race.

November 7, 1972

Nixon Reelected

Republican Richard Nixon is re-elected president, crushing Democrat George McGovern in the presidental election of 1972.

January 27, 1973

Vietnam Peace

The Paris Peace Treaty establishes a ceasefire in Vietnam.

September 11, 1973

Chile Coup

In Chile, the military bombs the presidential palace, overthrowing the elected left-wing government of Salvador Allende, who is either murdered or commits suicide. Army commander Augusto Pinochet installs himself as dictator.

October 6, 1973

Yom Kippur War

The Yom Kippur War begins as Egyptian and Syrian troops, using Soviet tanks, cross the Suez

Canal to launch a surprise attack against Israel on the Jewish Yom Kippur holiday. Israel requests arms from the United States, and the Americans attempt to send them; however, European countries (except for Portugal) refuse to let the Americans use air bases on their soil for this purpose. Egyptian President Anwar Sadat temporarily regains the territory his country lost in the Six-Day War of 1967, but will not then accept a ceasefire, continuing the war. Israeli forces recover from their initial setbacks, counterattacking to retake the land captured by Egypt. Secretary of State Henry Kissinger puts America's nuclear weapons on DEFCON III, an unprecedented level of high-alert.

October 22, 1973

Yom Kippur Resolution

United Nations Security Council Resolution 338, coauthored by American Secretary of State Henry Kissinger and Soviet Premier Leonid Brezhnev, calls for a ceasefire to end the Yom Kippur War.

October 19, 1973

OPEC Imposes Oil Embargo

The Organization of Petroleum Exporting Countries (OPEC), led by Saudi King Faisal, imposes an oil embargo on the United States and other Western powers in retaliation for their support of Israel during the Yom Kippur War.

October 27, 1973

Peace Talks Begin

Egypt and Israel begin peace talks to end the Yom Kippur War. Leaders from both countries meet at Kilometer 101, a point of passage between the two nations located between Cairo and the Suez Canal.

November 11, 1973

Yom Kippur Peace Treaty Reached

An agreement ending the Yom Kippur War is reached between Egypt and Israel, and the US resumes diplomatic relations with Egypt. Still, the Organization of Petroleum Exporting

Countries (OPEC) continues its oil embargo against the US. American oil prices skyrocket by 400% in 1974.

November 23, 1974

SALT II
President Gerald Ford and Soviet Premier Leonid Brezhnev meet in Vladivostok to sign accords limiting offensive nuclear weapons. This lays the groundwork for another Strategic Arms Limitation Treaty (SALT II), which further restricts the arms held by both nations.

March 17, 1974

Oil Embargo Ends
The Organization of Petroleum Exporting Countries (OPEC) ends its oil embargo against the United States.

1975

Cold War Stable
1975 marks the high point of détente between the United States and Soviet Union. The Vietnam War is over, China is America's friend, relations between East and West Germany are improving, and the US and USSR have made a number of agreements to slow the nuclear arms race. The Cold War seems to have stabilized, with reduced tensions on both sides.

People

Lyndon B. Johnson

Lyndon B. Johnson (1908-1973) was the 36th president of the United States, assuming the office after the assassination of President John F. Kennedy in November 1963. Prior to serving as Kennedy's vice president, Johnson had long represented Texas in the United States Senate.

Johnson inherited Kennedy's foreign policy and most of his advisers. Believing he was carrying out Kennedy's legacy, Johnson massively escalated American involvement in the Vietnam War.

John F. Kennedy

John F. Kennedy (1917-1963) was the 35th president of the United States. Elected in 1960 at the age of 43, he became the youngest person ever to be voted into the White House. Kennedy served from 1961 until his assassination in November 1963. To this day, many Americans remember Kennedy as an idealistic champion of freedom at home and abroad, despite the fact that his policies on civil rights, Vietnam, and Cuba sometimes failed to live up to his soaring rhetoric.

In the 1960 presidential campaign, Kennedy positioned himself to the right of the Republican Eisenhower Administration by promising to close the "missile gap," the supposed Soviet superiority in long-range nuclear missiles. In fact, Kennedy's "missile gap" charges were false; the US always had many times more intercontinental ballistic missiles than the Soviets. Still, Kennedy's promises of a strong and aggressive Cold War posture appealed to voters, who narrowly elected him over vice president Richard Nixon. Kennedy's reputation as a strong Cold Warrior soon ran aground in Cuba, where he was humiliated in the 1961 Bay of Pigs Invasion and where the 1962 Cuban Missile Crisis nearly led to nuclear holocaust. Spooked by the near-disaster of the Missile Crisis, Kennedy subsequently pursued more moderate policies with regard to the Soviet Union.

Henry Kissinger

Henry Kissinger (1923-) was the powerful National Security Advisor to president Richard Nixon and then became Secretary of State during Nixon's second term. Kissinger was among the most powerful presidential advisers in American history, shaping nearly all foreign policy decisions made under Nixon's tenure.

Kissinger's strategy for policymaking tended to rely on setting up meetings through back channels, thus fitting with Nixon's preference for secrecy. A crafty and even Machiavellian master of diplomacy, Kissinger paved the way for Nixon to visit China by making an earlier trip there himself. He also helped to negotiate peace in the Middle East following the Yom Kippur War.

Robert S. McNamara

Robert McNamara (1916-) is an American business executive, statesman, and diplomat. In 1960, he left his seat as president of the Ford Motor Company to accept an invitation from President Kennedy to become U.S. Secretary of Defense. A key adviser to the president during the Cuban Missile Crisis, McNamara is most famous (or infamous) today as the prime architect of the disastrous American intervention in the Vietnam War.

In the early 1960s, McNamara developed the idea of Mutual Assured Destruction, which held that in a world in which both the US and USSR possessed enough nuclear weapons to wipe each other off the map, both sides' fears of nuclear retaliation would prevent either from ever using the weapons for aggressive purposes. Thus nuclear weapons were the best deterrent against nuclear war. Although critics decried McNamara's nuclear "balance of terror" policy as mad (MAD, conveniently, was the acronym for Mutual Assured Destruction), McNamara believed his policy would help maintain a stable nuclear world.

Richard M. Nixon

Richard M. Nixon (1913 - 1994) was a Republican senator from California and the thirty-seventh president of the United States. Prior to his presidency, he also served as Dwight Eisenhower's Vice President from 1953 to 1961. Ultimately, his presidency ended in disgrace, with Nixon's 1974 resignation in the midst of the Watergate scandal.

Nixon built his early political career almost entirely around the issue of anticommunism. He rode his reputation as an aggressive foe of Communism at home and abroad to the US Senate and the vice presidency. As president, however, Nixon changed course. With the aid of his National Security Advisor and (later) Secretary of State Henry Kissinger, Nixon moderated his strong anticommunist views, surprising the world by pursuing détente with the Soviet Union and opening diplomatic relations with Red China.

Did You Know?

Trivia

"Ich bin ein Berliner," said President John F. Kennedy in 1963, expressing his solidarity with the beleaguered citizens of Berlin in a famous speech delivered there soon after East Germany built the Berlin Wall. But Kennedy was no native speaker of German; a true Berliner would have said simply, "Ich bin Berliner." Some have argued that, by using the article "ein," Kennedy accidentally declared himself to be a type of jelly doughnut. But there is no evidence that anyone heard his speech that way at the time; Kennedy's message of solidarity was clear, even if his German grammar was rudimentary.

When John F. Kennedy campaigned in 1960 on the issue of the "missile gap," there did exist a gap... but it overwhelmingly favored the United States. The actual count of intercontinental ballistic missiles in 1961: the Soviets had about 10 instead of the 1000 feared[6], and the Americans had 57.[7]

Key Quotes

"Ich bin ein Berliner."

– John F. Kennedy, speech in Berlin, 1963 [8]

"We're eyeball to eyeball, and I think the other fellow just blinked."

– Secretary of State Dean Rusk, during the Cuban Missile Crisis, 1962 [9]

"Let every nation know, whether it wishes us well or ill, that we shall pay any price, bear any burden, meet any hardship, support any friend, oppose any foe, to assure the survival and the success of liberty.... Let us never negotiate out of fear, but let us never fear to negotiate. Let both sides explore what problems unite us instead of belaboring those problems which divide us.... And so, my fellow Americans, ask not what your country can do for you; ask what you can do for your country. My fellow citizens of the world, ask not what America will do for you, but what together we can do for the freedom of man."

– John F. Kennedy, inaugural address, 1961 [10]

"The week that changed the world."

– Richard M. Nixon, on his visit to China, 1972 [11]

"It's not mad! Mutual Assured Destruction is the foundation of deterrence."

– Secretary of Defense Robert S. McNamara [12]

"It was a perfectly beautiful night, as fall nights are in Washington. I walked out of the president's Oval Office, and as I walked out, I thought I might never live to see another Saturday night."

– Secretary of Defense Robert S. McNamara, recalling the Cuban Missile Crisis [13]

Statistics

Number of warheads in the American nuclear arsenal in 1959: 15,468
Number of warheads in the American nuclear arsenal in 1960: 20,434
Number of warheads in the American nuclear arsenal in 1961: 24,156
Number of warheads in the American nuclear arsenal in 1962: 27,305
Number of warheads in the American nuclear arsenal in 1963: 29,049
Number of warheads in the American nuclear arsenal in 1964: 30,400
Number of warheads in the American nuclear arsenal in 1965: 31,265
Number of warheads in the American nuclear arsenal in 1966: 31,323
Number of warheads in the American nuclear arsenal in 1967: 30,516
Number of warheads in the American nuclear arsenal in 1968: 28,507
Number of warheads in the American nuclear arsenal in 1969: 26,533
Number of warheads in the American nuclear arsenal in 1970: 25,742
Number of warheads in the American nuclear arsenal in 1971: 25,988
Number of warheads in the American nuclear arsenal in 1972: 26,919
Number of warheads in the American nuclear arsenal in 1973: 27,958
Number of warheads in the American nuclear arsenal in 1974: 27,793
Number of warheads in the American nuclear arsenal in 1975: 26,675
Number of warheads in the American nuclear arsenal in 1976: 25,579
Number of warheads in the American nuclear arsenal in 1977: 24,722
Number of warheads in the American nuclear arsenal in 1978: 23,866
Number of warheads in the American nuclear arsenal in 1979: 23,730
Number of warheads in the American nuclear arsenal in 1980: 23,387

American aid to Israel in 1970: $71 million
American aid to Israel in 1973: $467 million
American aid to Israel in 1974: $2.6 billion

From 1964 to 1970, US defense spending never fell below 40% of the total federal budget.
From 1970 to 1980, US defense spending steadily decreased as a portion of the federal budget
from 40% to 23%.

In 1974, during the OPEC oil embargo, oil prices in the US increased by 400%.

On 30 October 1961, a Russian bomber dropped the Tsar Bomb, the largest nuclear weapon
ever detonated. The Tsar Bomb's force was equal to 50 million tons of TNT, making it
thousands of times more powerful than the atomic bomb dropped on Hiroshima in 1945.

Acronyms

ARVN: Army of the Republic of Vietnam (South Vietnam)
CIA: Central Intelligence Agency
DMZ: Demilitarized Zone
DRV: Democratic Republic of Vietnam (North Vietnam)
ExComm: Executive Committee
FRG: Federal Republic of Germany (West Germany)
GDR: German Democratic Republic (East Germany)
ICBM: Intercontinental Ballistic Missile
KGB: Committee for State Security (Soviet secret police and espionage agency)
NATO: North Atlantic Treaty Organization
NSC: National Security Council
NLF: National Liberation Front for South Vietnam (a.k.a. Viet Cong, a communist guerilla army fighting against the USA and South Vietnamese government during the Vietnam War)
OPEC: Organization of Petroleum Exporting Countries
MAD: Mutual Assured Destruction
RVN: Republic of Vietnam (South Vietnam)
SALT: Strategic Arms Limitation Treaty
UN: United Nations
USSR: Union of Soviet Socialist Republics (Soviet Union)

Glossary

arms race
A competition between rival nations to achieve superiority in military weaponry.

bipolar
An international system in which two rival superpowers dominate global affairs. The Cold War, in which the world was essentially divided into two hostile camps respectively aligned with the United States and Soviet Union, epitomized bipolar international politics.

Cold War
The decades-long confrontation between the United States and the Soviet Union, which lasted from the late 1940s to the early 1990s. The name "Cold War" arose from the fact that the conflict that never escalated to direct military confrontation (that would have been a "hot war").

capitalism, capitalist
A socio-economic system in which property and the means of production are owned by private citizens or corporations rather than by the state. Decentralized market behavior, rather than centralized government decision-making, determines the allocation of goods through society.

Communism

A social, political, and economic system rooted in the philosophies of Karl Marx and V.I. Lenin, in which all economic and social activity is controlled by the state and/or the Communist Party. All property is owned collectively; there is no private property or private enterprise.

containment

An American policy that sought to halt the spread of Communism to countries which were not already Communist.

détente, detente

A relaxation of tensions between hostile nations.

Iron Curtain

The line that divided Soviet-dominated Eastern Europe from Western Europe. Former British Prime Minister Winston Churchill coined the phrase in a 1946 speech.

Kremlin, the Kremlin

A fortified palace complex at the heart of Moscow, the Kremlin is the seat of power of the Russian government. "The Kremlin" was often used as a shorthand to refer to the entire Soviet government, as in: "The Kremlin objected to the Marshall Plan."

Massive Retaliation

A military doctrine announced by President Eisenhower's Secretary of State, John Foster Dulles, in 1954, Massive Retaliation was meant to deter Communist aggression by suggesting that any Communist provocation, anywhere in the world, could lead to massive retaliation—a nuclear strike—by the United States against the Soviet Union itself.

Moscow

The capital of Russia and the Soviet Union. "Moscow" is often used as a shorthand for the Soviet government, as in: "Moscow sent in troops."

multipolar

An international system in which many powerful states exert significant influence on global affairs.

proxy war, proxy wars

A war in which two superpowers support opposing third parties as a substitute for fighting each other directly. For example, Angola's Civil War during the 1970s was a prominent proxy war of the Cold War era. The Soviet Union and Cuba backed the Marxist MPLA government, while the United States and South Africa backed the anticommuist UNITA rebels.

self-determination

The principle that the citizens of a nation should be able to choose their own form of government through democratic processes.

Soviet satellite, Soviet satellites
A nation that was formally independent, but in fact dominated by and subservient to the Soviet Union. After World War II, many of the nations of Eastern Europe became Soviet satellites.

Third World
A term used to describe poor, underdeveloped nations—usually former colonies of European powers—in Africa, Asia, and Latin America. During the Cold War, the United States and the Soviet Union each sought to win allies in the Third World.

The West
In the context of the Cold War, "the West" referred to the anticommunist nations of Western Europe and North America, which joined together in formal military alliance through the North Atlantic Treaty Organization (NATO). The West existed in contrast to the Communist nations of the East.

Best of the Web

Books
John Lewis Gaddis, *The Cold War: A New History* (2005)
The most recent interpretation of Cold War events by historian John Gaddis.

David Reynolds, *One World Divisible, A Global History since 1945* (2000)
A detailed textbook history of the Cold War.

Margaret MacMillan, *Nixon and Mao: The Week that Changed the World* (2007)
A detailed account of the meetings between Nixon and Mao in China.

Robert F. Kennedy and Arthur Schlesinger, Jr., *Thirteen Days: A Memoir of the Cuban Missile Crisis* (1969)
An insider's look at the Cuban Missile Crisis from the point of view of Robert F. Kennedy.

Movies & TV
Topaz (1969)
One of Alfred Hitchcock's lesser-known films, *Topaz* is a fictional depiction of the circumstances surrounding the Cuban Missile Crisis. In this Cold War thriller a Russian official defects to the U.S. and reveals both a pro-Soviet French spy ring and a secret alliance between

the Soviets and the Cubans. Not good. It's up to U.S. secret agent Michael Nordstrom and his French sidekick to prevent a full-blown nuclear war. Perhaps not one of Hitchcock's best films, *Topaz* is worth seeing, if only to observe the way the director has chosen to depict each of the regimes involved in the 1962 crisis.

d War. It's a sobering peak at the complicated, imperfect, and uncertain decisions that can and do lead to war.br /br /a href="http://www.imdb.com/title/tt0343737/"target="_blank"> *The Good Shepherd* (2006)
A recent Hollywood film featuring Brangelina, *Good Shepherd* is about the history of the U.S. Central Intelligence Service (CIA). See Brad Pitt struggle to be a good son, a loyal husband, and a dedicated father all while trying to help save the post-World War II world from nuclear war. (That's quite a plateful!)

Music
Bob Dylan, *Willy and the Poor Boys* (1969)
The fourth album from an iconic American band, *Willy and the Poor Boys* is chock full of CCR classics including "Down on the Corner,"the anti-Vietnam anthem "Fortunate Son," and "It Came Out of the Sky," a song that seemed to warn of a war far more destructive than the one in Southeast Asia.

George Clinton, *1999* (1983)
You may have partied "like it's 1999"recently. You may even have partied "like it's 1999" *in* 1999. But have you considered that Prince's iconic song, released in 1983, was actually a Cold War apocalyptic anthem?

U2,
Photos & Pics
Aerial Espionage
http://www.gwu.edu/~nsarchiv/NSAEBB/NSAEBB13/1.jpg
Satellite reconnaissance images of a Soviet airfield

JFK & LBJ
http://www.jfklibrary.org/Asset+Tree/Asset+Viewers/Image+Asset+Viewer.htm?guid={63BCD66 2-D21C-4D45-AE33-05A49CB9AB8E}&type=Image
President Kennedy and Vice President Johnson walking to a ceremony on the South Lawn

Inside ExComm
http://www.jfklibrary.org/Asset+Tree/Asset+Viewers/Image+Asset+Viewer.htm?guid={68EEE04 9-5AD1-499A-8A69-7A0CE1056715}&type=Image
Photo of an ExComm meeting during the Cuban Missile Crisis

Nixon Goes to China
http://www.gmu.edu/library/specialcollections/acsnic6_12_1f.jpg

President Richard Nixon meets Chinese Communist leader Mao Zedong

Ping Pong Diplomacy
http://www.gmu.edu/library/specialcollections/acsnic6_14_20f.jpg
The Nixons and Chinese Communist leader Zhou Enlai applaud a table tennis exhibition

Historical Documents
Cold War Documents
http://www.yale.edu/lawweb/avalon/coldwar.htm
Yale Avalon Project—Cold War Documents: A collection of documents organized in categories of events and then in chronological order so you can piece together what unfolds.

More Cold War Documents
http://www.mtholyoke.edu/acad/intrel/coldwar.htm
Documents Related to the Cold War: A well-organized list hosted by Mt. Holyoke Collegeof links and documents relating to the Cold War, organized by year of event.

Still More Cold War Documents
http://www.wilsoncenter.org/index.cfm?topic_id=1409&fuseaction=va2.browse&sort=Collection
Cold War International History Project at the Wilson Center: A large archive of documents with an international focus.

Secret Cold War Documents
http://www.gwu.edu/~nsarchiv/
National Security Archive: Collection of secret government documents, received via the Freedom of Information Act.

Presidential Papers
http://www.presidency.ucsb.edu/ws/
American Presidency Project: A collection of the public papers of American presidents.

Video
JFK Audio
http://www.jfklibrary.org/Historical+Resources/Archives/Reference+Desk/Speeches/
Audio recordings of Kennedy's speeches

Nixon in China
http://nixon.archives.gov/virtuallibrary/tapeexcerpts/chinatapes.php
Audio recordings of Nixon's speeches about his visit to China

Nixon Foreign Policy
http://nixon.archives.gov/virtuallibrary/tapeexcerpts/tapeexcerpts.php
Conversations between Nixon and others related to foreign affairs

http://www.americanrhetoric.com/speeches/jfkinaugural.htm
Video of Kennedy's inaugural address

Websites

CNN's Cold War
http://www.cnn.com/SPECIALS/cold.war/
The website for CNN's documentary miniseries *The Cold War* contains transcripts of the program and a wealth of additional materials. One of America's leading Cold War historians, Yale professor John Lewis Gaddis, consulted on the program.

Cold War Museum
http://www.coldwar.org/
The Cold War Museum is a touring exhibit about the Cold War, dedicated to honoring Cold War veterans. One of the museum's founders is Francis Gary Powers, Jr., son of the pilot Francis Gary Powers who was shot down in his U2 spy plane over Russia in 1960.

Kennedy Library
http://www.jfklibrary.org
The John F. Kennedy Presidential Library contains collections of presidential papers with documents, photographs, and speeches online.

Johnson Library
http://www.lbjlib.utexas.edu
The Lyndon B. Johnson Presidential Library contains collections of presidential papers with documents, photographs, and speeches online.

National Security Archive
http://www.gwu.edu/~nsarchiv/
The National Security Archive uses the federal Freedom of Information Act to obtain secret government documents from the Cold War era. Great collection of articles and documents related to national security.

Test Review

People

Lyndon B. Johnson
- Democratic President of the United States, 1963-1969
- John F. Kennedy's Vice President, took office after assassination, then won full term of his own in 1964 elections

- Escalated American involvement in Vietnam War
- Enacted sweeping domestic reforms, but presidency ruined by disaster in Vietnam

John F. Kennedy
- Democratic President of the United States, 1961-63
- Won election on strong Cold War platform, promising to close nonexistent "missile gap" with Soviets
- Ordered failed Bay of Pigs invasion against Castro's Cuba, then performed much better in leading U.S. through Cuban Missile Crisis
- Oversaw early stages of Vietnam War, but his future policy on Vietnam was unclear at time of his assassination in 1963

Henry Kissinger
- Powerful National Security Advisor and then Secretary of State under Presidents Nixon and Ford
- Shaped virtually all of Nixon's foreign policy decisions, including strategy of détente
- Organized Nixon's groundbreaking visit to China, helped reduce Cold War tensions in 1970s

Robert S. McNamara
- Secretary of Defense under Presidents Kennedy and Johnson
- Prime architect of Vietnam War, heavily criticized by antiwar activists
- Also helped guide Kennedy through Cuban Missile Crisis, 1962
- Eventually lost faith in his own Vietnam policy and either quit or was fired from Johnson Administration

Richard M. Nixon
- Republican President of the United States, 1969-74
- Resigned in disgrace in wake of Watergate scandal, 1974
- Strong anticommunist throughout his career, but adopted more flexible approach as President
- At Kissinger's urging, pursued détente with U.S.S.R. and opened diplomatic relations with China

Nikita Khrushchev
- Soviet leader following Stalin's death, 1953
- Initially more open to dialogue with West and within Soviet sphere
- Denounced Stalin's crimes in secret speech to Soviet leadership, 1956
- Adopted a harder line against West after 1960; led Soviet Union during Cuban Missile Crisis

Mao Zedong
- Leader of Chinese Communists, defeated Nationalists in Civil War in 1949; ruled Red China until his death in 1976
- Ordered Chinese troops to intervene against Americans in Korean War

- Called atom bomb "paper tiger" or meaningless threat in early 1950s
- Established friendly relations with Richard Nixon in 1970s

Alexander Dubcek
- Reformist leader of Czechoslovakia's Communist Party during "Prague Spring"
- Desired "socialism with a human face," a type of Communism that allowed greater individual freedom
- Removed from power through Soviet invasion of Czechoslovakia, 1968

Events

1959 Castro's Revolution in Cuba
- Leftist guerillas led by young Fidel Castro toppled autocratic, pro-American government in Cuba
- Castro did not take power as a Communist, but as relations with U.S. soured, he soon established alliance with U.S.S.R.

1961 Bay of Pigs Disaster
- President Kennedy authorized invasion of Cuba by anti-Castro exiles
- Invasion ended in disastrous failure, undermining Kennedy at home and abroad
- Made Soviet leader Khrushchev believe Kennedy was weak and inexperienced and could be bullied

1962 Cuban Missile Crisis
- U.S. discovered Soviet installation of nuclear missiles in Cuba
- Americans "quarantined" (blockaded) island, demanded withdrawal of missiles
- After 13 days of intense negotiations, Soviet missiles were withdrawn in exchange for U.S. removal of missiles in Turkey and pledged never to invade Cuba again
- American people, not informed of agreement, believed that Kennedy had won through hard line and not negotiation
- Closest world ever came to nuclear annihilation

1964 Gulf of Tokin Incident
- U.S. Navy ship allegedly attacked near North Vietnamese waters
- It remains unclear whether there was any actual attack or whether it was a false alarm
- Used as pretext to justify congressional resolution authorizing full-blown intervention of American ground troops in Vietnam

1968 Prague Spring
- Dubcek proposed "socialism with a human face", encouraging greater freedoms for citizens
- Ruthlessly crushed by Soviets

- Soviets adopted Brezhnev Doctrine, dictating that no socialist state would be allowed to liberalize institutions or U.S.S.R. would intervene with force

1969 Strategic Arms Limitation Treaty (SALT) Negotiations Begin
- Nuclear arms reduction treaty signed by U.S. and U.S.S.R. in 1972
- Limited number of ballistic missiles held by either side at current levels
- Marked formal beginning of détente

1972 Nixon Goes to China
- Ends 23-year-old policy of American non-recognition of Red China
- Establishment of relations with U.S. drove wedge further between U.S.S.R. and China, dividing Communist world into two camps

Groups

Organization of Petroleum Exporting Countries (OPEC)
- Oil cartel, originally composed of Iraq, Iran, Kuwait, Saudi Arabia, Venezuela
- Attempted to coordinate oil production and pricing
- Imposed oil boycott on U.S. In wake of 1973 Yom Kippur War in Israel
- Demonstrated American reliance on foreign oil, potential problems dealing with Third World

Concepts

Détente
- Policy of relaxation of tensions between U.S. and U.S.S.R.
- Pursued by Kissinger, détente began with SALT I treaty, peaked in 1975
- Dominated "middle period" of Cold War, following tense early 1960s and preceding tense early 1980s

Brinksmanship
- Practice of pushing conflict to brink of disaster in order to force opponent to relent
- Practiced by Cold War leaders in Washington and Moscow in Cuban Missile Crisis, Berlin Airlift

Mutual Assured Destruction
- Concept that the best deterrent against nuclear war was the guarantee that a nation that launched a first strike would be destroyed by enemy's nuclear retaliation; thus any launch was completely irrational
- Concept developed by McNamara
- Weakness was that policymaking during international crises wasn't always rational

Places

Bay of Pigs, Cuba
- Site of failed invasion by American-backed exiles hoping to topple Castro's regime in Cuba, 1961

Prague, Czechoslovakia
- Czech capital was site of 1968 "Prague Spring," an effort to reform Communism to allow greater individual freedoms
- Reform movement ended with crushing Soviet military invasion of city

Citations

[1] "China," Cold War, episode 15, CNN Presents, original broadcast 24 January 1999, http://www.cnn.com/SPECIALS/cold.war/episodes/15/script.html, accessed 1 December 2008.

[2] "Ping-Pong Diplomacy (April 6 - 17, 1971)," Nixon's China Game, The American Experience, PBS, http://www.pbs.org/wgbh/amex/china/peopleevents/pande07.html, accessed 1 December 2008.

[3] "China," CNN presents "Cold War," episode 15, original broadcast 24 January 1999, http://www.cnn.com/SPECIALS/cold.war/episodes/15/script.html, accessed 1 December 2008.

[4] John F. Kennedy, "Excerpts of Speech by Senator John F. Kennedy, American Legion Convention, Miami Beach, FL - (Advance Release Text), " delivered 18 October 1960, Miami Beach, FL, archived by The American Presidency Project, UC Santa Barbara, http://www.presidency.ucsb.edu/ws/index.php?pid=74095, accessed 1 December 2008.

[5] John Lewis Gaddis, We Now Know: Rethinking Cold War History (Oxford: OUP, 1998), 241.

[6] "Table of USSR/Russian ICBM Forces," Archive of Nuclear Data, Natural Resources Defense Council, Nuclear Program, http://www.nrdc.org/nuclear/nudb/datab4.asp, accessed 1 December 2008.

[7] "Table of US ICBM Forces," Archive of Nuclear Data, Natural Resources Defense Council, Nuclear Program, http://www.nrdc.org/nuclear/nudb/datab3.asp, accessed 1 December 2008.

[8] John F Kennedy, "Ich bin ein Berliner," speech delivered 26 June 1963, West Berlin, Germany, archived by American Rhetoric, http://www.americanrhetoric.com/speeches/jfkberliner.html, accessed 1 December 2008.

[9] Thomas Blanton, "Annals of Blinksmanship," The Wilson Quarterly (Summer: 1997), The National Security Archives: George Washington University, http://www.gwu.edu/~nsarchiv/nsa/cuba_mis_cri/annals.htm, accessed 1 December 2008.

[10] John F Kennedy, "Inagural Address," speech delivered 20 January 1963, Washington, DC, archieved by American Rhetoric, http://www.americanrhetoric.com/speeches/jfkinaugural.htm, accessed 1 December 2008.

[11] "The Nixon Visit - (February 21-28, 1972)," Nixon's China Game, The American Experience, PBS, http://www.pbs.org/wgbh/amex/china/sfeature/nixon.html, accessed 1 December 2008.

[12] ""MAD," Cold War, episode 12, CNN Presents, originally broadcast 13 December 1998, http://www.cnn.com/SPECIALS/cold.war/episodes/12/script.html, accessed 1 December 2008.

[13] "Cuba," Cold War, episode 10, CNN Presents, originally broadcast 29 November 1998, http://www.cnn.com/SPECIALS/cold.war/episodes/10/script.html, accessed 1 December 2008.